20 DAY FORGIVENESS JOURNAL

See yourself in a new light as you transform your thoughts so you can release unforgiveness & receive love more completely

Beth Brown

Copyright © 2022 Beth Brown.

All rights reserved. No part of this book may be reproduced, stored, or transmitted by any means—whether auditory, graphic, mechanical, or electronic—without written permission of both publisher and author, except in the case of brief excerpts used in critical articles and reviews. Unauthorized reproduction of any part of this work is illegal and is punishable by law.

A FEW TIPS FOR SUCCESSFUL JOURNALING:

- Commit to a specific time each day to reflect & journal for 20 minutes
- Choose a comfortable & non-distracting location in your home to journal in
- Turn your phone off or set it on airplane mode to block outside distractions from reaching you
- Have a fancy pen or pencil on hand that makes journaling more enjoyable
- For 1:1 forgiveness coaching e-mail levelupwithbeth@gmail.com

© Beth Brown 2022
1st edition 2022
Contact: levelupwithbeth@gmail.com

DAY 1

Self-Awareness - Observing Your Thoughts without Self-Judgment

Journal about the first thought(s) you had when you woke up today.

DAY 2

Anxiety release activity

As you go through this journal challenge, there may be moments when you have emotional experiences of anxiety or fear come up. This is because our muscles have memories. They remember both our good & bad experiences. It's not so much about erasing memories in our minds, but creating new memories for our bodies & our minds to remember. Today practice restoring your body to a place of peace.

Place both hands gently over the area of your body experiencing anxiety or the area that typically experiences anxious energy. Massage the area & speak loving words to your body. Tell your body that right now it is in a safe place.

Journal how you experienced this activity.

DAY 3
Musical Healing

Listen to the song Psalms 139 (Far Too Wonderful) by Shane & Shane. Journal your thoughts, impressions, emotions, etc. about the song.

https://www.youtube.com/watch?v=uQYnIM80PtQ

DAY 4

Scriptural Healing - Philippians $: 6-9 (NIV)

"Do not be anxious about anything, but in every situation, by prayer and petition, with thanksgiving present your requests to God. And the peace of God, which transcends all understanding will guard your hearts and your minds in Christ Jesus."

"Finally, brothers and sisters, whatever is true, whatever is noble, whatever is right, whatever is pure, whatever is lovely, whatever is admirable - if anything is excellent or praiseworthy - think about such things. Whatever you have learned from me, or seen in me - put it into practice. And the God of peace will be with you."

Journal your thoughts about the words or phrases that stood out to you. Journal the emotions you experienced as you read these verses. Journal your requests to God, just like the author of Philippians suggests.

Suggestion: As you are writing out your requests, simultaneously read them aloud.

DAY 5

Self Awareness - Brain Dump

Increase your self-awareness about how you are focusing your thoughts after the weekend.

Set a timer for 5 minutes. Begin writing everything that is currently on your mind. If possible write in one continuous conscious stream without lifting your pen off the paper.

When the timer goes off, take the paper, ball it up & symbolically release what's been weighing on your mind by tossing the paper away in the trash.

DAY 6

Worry Release

Sometimes we hold back forgiving ourselves or someone else because we are worried about what might happen if we forgive.

Take 20 minutes to release everything you are worried might happen if you choose to forgive the person or people who hurt you.

Then pray your journal entry back to God & release your worries to him, trusting him to remember & take care of you.

DAY 7

Musical Healing

Listen to the song **Be Okay** by Zoe Music. Journal your thoughts, impressions, emotions, etc. about the song.

https://www.youtube.com/watch?v=fVtySBw-c8w

DAY 8

Scriptural Healing - Hebrews 10:35

"Cast not away therefore your confidence, which hath great recompense of reward."

Journal your thoughts about the words or phrases that stood out to you. Journal the emotions you experienced as you read these verses. Journal your recompense requests to God.

Suggestion: Include in your recompense prayer request a commitment to trusting God's promise to give you great recompense for your pain & loss. Then as you go about your day & week keep an eye out for the miracle recompense moments he will be bringing your way.

DAY 9

Work It Out

Imagine yourself breaking free from the anger, grief, betrayal, shame, etc. whatever emotions have been holding you back from being able to forgive yourself, someone else or even God.

After dancing, journal for 5 minutes about your visualizations & about how your body & mind feels after the dance workout.

If you need some dance inspiration, here are 2 YouTube options:

Official Boss Fam
https://www.youtube.com/channel/UCXipBJpeaa_Zt7K9ePxA6Jg

Kyra Pro
https://www.youtube.com/c/KyraPro

DAY 10

Self Awareness - Anger Release

Oftentimes we bottle our anger up, especially if our anger is against someone we feel ashamed or fearful of being angry with, this is especially true for Christians who feel angry at God. Write an honest letter to who you are angry at. (yourself, a person, God) After writing, ball up the letter & release your anger symbolically by tossing it out.

DAY 11

Breath Release

Breathing Techniques:

When hyper stressed – inhale 2 short breaths, exhale long breath

When needing energy – inhale long breath, exhale short breath

Suggestion: Do today's journaling activity at the end of the day.

Pay attention to your breathing as you have different thoughts pass through your mind, interact with different people, find yourself in different settings, etc. Journal your noticings about your breathing patterns.

DAY 12

Musical Healing

Listen to the song **I'll Find You** by Lecrae (feat. Tori Kelly) Journal your thoughts, impressions, emotions, etc. about the song.

https://www.youtube.com/watch?v=bPsr7Y6TQRY

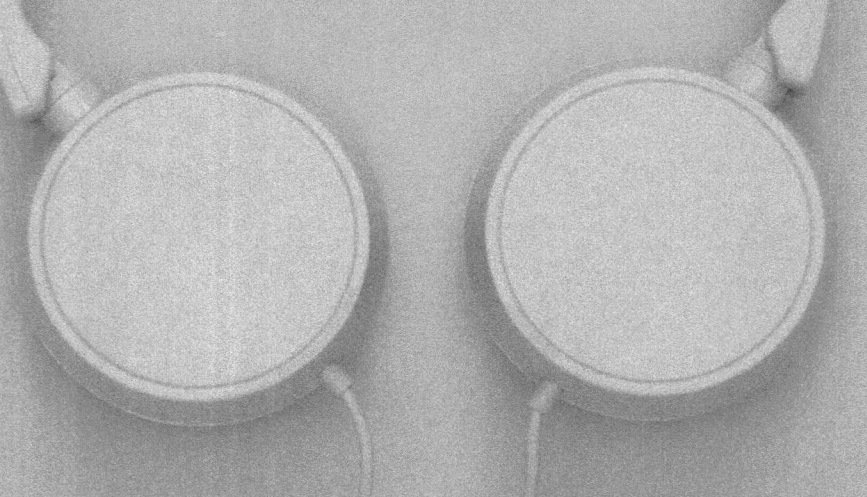

DAY 13

Scriptural Healing - Psalms 139: 17 - 18 (AMP)

"How precious also are Your thoughts to me, O God! How vast is the sum of them! If I could count them, they would outnumber the sand. When I awake, I am still with You."

Journal your thoughts about the words or phrases that stood out to you. Journal the emotions you experienced as you read these verses.

Suggestion: In your journal entry, ask God to share with you some of his precious thoughts about you. Thank him for always being with you, even during your darkest moments when you felt alone, betrayed, rejected, etc.

DAY 14

Declutter

Do you still have physical memories of the person or life event that hurt you? (e.g. Do you still have text messages in your phone from a nasty breakup? Are you holding onto songs in your playlists that remind you of the person who hurt you or that when you listen to make you feel sad, angry, etc?)

Take 20 minutes today to declutter your phone of memories that return you to the place of pain.

Journal about what you decluttered & what you plan to toss out at a later date when you have more time to clear things out. Journal how you felt or feel about decluttering.

DAY 15

Self Awareness – Love Release

Write a love letter or a love poem to yourself.

Suggestion: Include in your letter or poem all the good things & freedoms you will experience in life if you choose forgiveness.

DAY 16

Stretch Release

Let's be honest, forgiving someone who has hurt us, particularly when the hurt was caused by someone we trusted to keep us safe is a HUGE stretch. Since our bodies hold memories in our muscles, this release is designed to create new, safe memories in our bodies.

As you stretch your body, visualize yourself stretching into the woman or man who you desire to be. Visualize yourself stretching free from the person or people who hurt you. Visualize yourself in a safe & loving space.

After stretching journal for 5 minutes about your visualizations & about how your body & mind feels after the stretch release.

Here are 2 YouTube options:

Crissy Mac - Full Body Stretches for beginners https://www.youtube.com/watch?v=689OKDEjIEU

Chloe Ting - Do This Warm Up Before Your Workouts https://www.youtube.com/watch?v=-p0PA9Zt8zk

DAY 17

Musical Healing

Listen to the song **Love is the More Excellent Way** by Babbie Mason. Journal your thoughts, impressions, emotions, etc. about the song.

https://www.youtube.com/watch?v=dM8BlynerKE

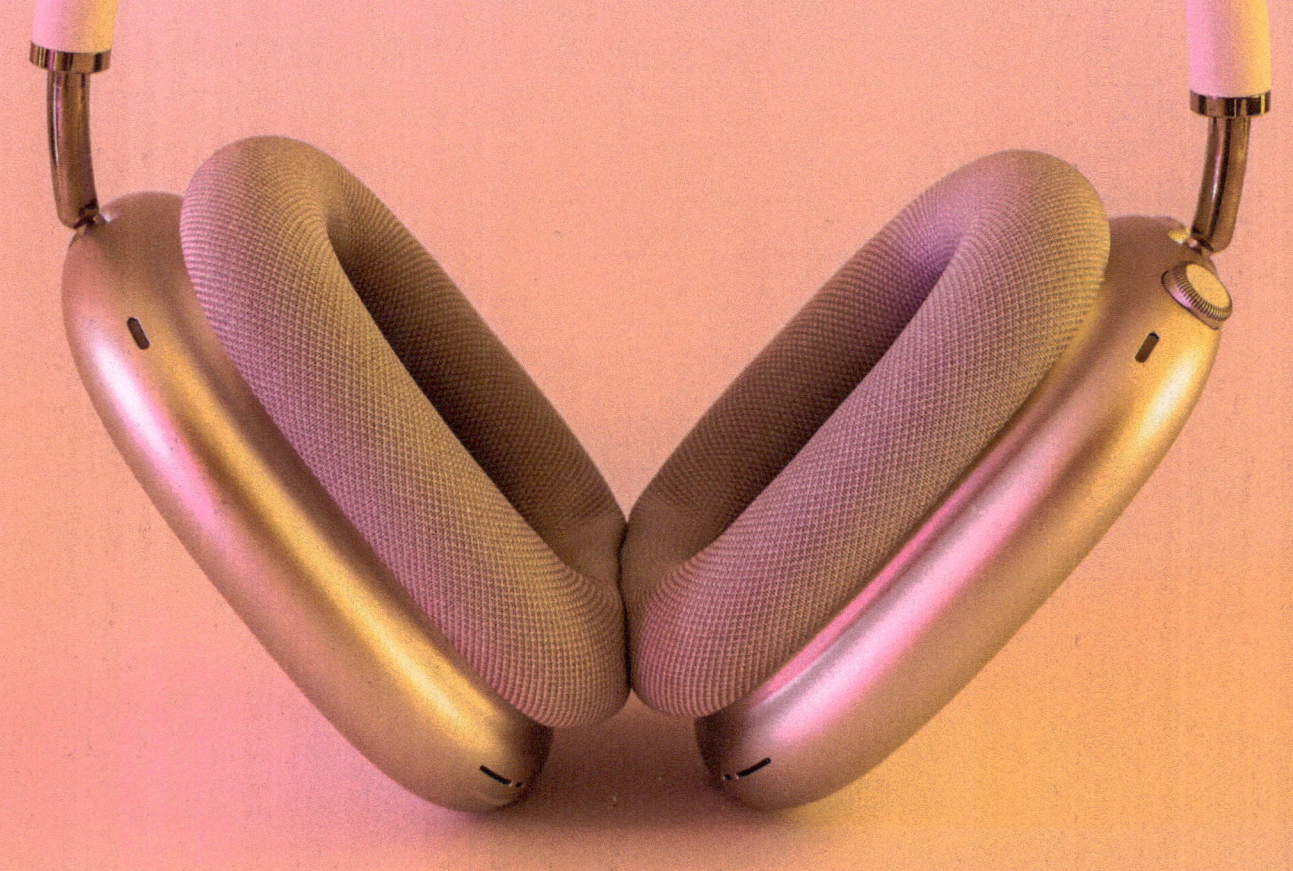

DAY 18

Scriptural Healing - Mark 11: 25 - 26 AMP

"Whenever you stand praying, if you have anything against anyone forgive him [drop the issue, let it go], so that your Father who is in heaven will also forgive you your transgressions and wrongdoings [against Him and others]. [But if you do not forgive, neither will your Father in heaven forgive your transgressions.]"

Journal your thoughts about the words or phrases that stood out to you. Journal the emotions you experienced as you read these verses.

Suggestion: In your journal ask God to forgive you for the anger, grudges, etc you have been holding onto. God is love & with love there is no fear. (1 John 4:18) This means he is a safe being who you can be honest with. If you want to forgive, but still don't feel ready, share your feelings with God & ask him to help you. There's no need to hide any reservations you have about forgiving someone from him. When you're open & honest, you open up space for your life transformation to begin.

DAY 19

Forgiveness Prayer

Dear Papa God,

Thank you for my life & for my future. Thank you that you made plans for me even before you laid the foundations of the earth. I know this pain I've been going through was not part of your plan for my life & I don't understand why you allowed it to happen to me, but I am choosing to trust your love to help me, to heal my emotions & relieve me of my pain, to help me not to judge myself or others in my heart & to give me great recompense for my pain & loss.

I know that your word says in Matthew 6:14 & 15 For if ye forgive men their trespasses, your heavenly Father will also forgive you: But if ye forgive not men their trespasses, neither will your Father forgive your trespasses.

continued on next page....

DAY 19

Forgiveness Prayer Continued

I don't want to be separated from you & the blessings you have for me any longer. I repent of the anger, bitterness, & judgemental complaints I have been holding against (insert person's name.) I release her/him from the debts she/he owes me. Forgive me for my unforgiving heart so that we can be cozy & comfortable friends again.

As I release (insert person's name) to you, I am trusting you, in your love & eternal wisdom, to manage everything as you know best. I am thankful that by forgiving (insert person's name) I can now live freely as the confident & strong woman/man who you created me to be. Lead me step by step through this process of healing & forgiving. In Jesus mighty & matchless name, Amen.

Journal suggestions: Write your own forgiveness prayer specific to your needs. Write how you felt during the time you were praying the forgiveness prayer & how you now feel after praying it.

DAY 20

Self-Awareness - Observing Thoughts without Self Judgement

What was the first thought(s) you had when you woke up today?

After you journal this morning's first thought go back & compare it with your Day 1 first thought(s). Is it lighter, more hopeful, the same, darker? Be sure to compare without self-judgement.

DID YOU ENJOY THE FORGIVENESS JOURNAL?

I'd love to hear how this 20 day forgiveness journal helped you release thoughts & emotions that have been weighting you down.

Please drop me an email or tag me on Instagram & share about your transformation.

Email: levelupwithbeth@gmail.com
Instagram: @babsphotographyllc

Interested in continuing to work together on transforming your life emotionally, spiritually & physically?

Email me at levelupwithbeth@gmail.com to learn if my self-love life transformational program **Seeing Myself in a New Light: Healing identity after trauma or heartbreak in 21 steps** is a good fit for you.

I'm proud of you for persisting to complete this journal. You made it through! I pray you will continue enjoying the new freedom you're experiencing as a result of releasing unforgiveness. Remember transformation is a continual process of progress.

www.ingramcontent.com/pod-product-compliance
Lightning Source LLC
Chambersburg PA
CBHW061808290426
44109CB00031B/2966